AF441260

Indoor Farming
for beginners

BRIAN TUNDLER

Copyright © 2020 Brian Tundler

All rights reserved.

ISBN: 9798622468575

to all the farmers

DEDICATION

to all the farmers

Contents

CHAPTER 1

Introducing Indoor Farming

Indoor farming is a strategy for developing harvests or plants, as a rule on an enormous scale, totally inside. This technique for cultivating regularly executes developing strategies, for example, hydroponics and uses fake lights to give plants the supplements and light levels required for development.

A wide assortment of plants can be developed inside, however natural products, vegetables, and herbs are the most mainstream.

Access to arable land and crisp water is declining, conventional business cultivating strategies are ecologically unsustainable and environmental change is getting to a lesser degree a danger and even more a reality. Notwithstanding these difficulties we should create enough nourishment to sustain a developing populace, a large number of whom are incessantly ravenous.

Some accept the appropriate response lies in an extreme change of our nourishment creation frameworks, to be specific indoor farming, a technique that can diminish the wastefulness and waste - for example of water or of yields - related with current cultivating rehearses.

Indoor farming is going on over the globe, albeit prevalently in created nations. The world's biggest indoor homestead at 25,000 square feet is situated in the old SONY industrial facility situated in eastern Japan's Miyagi Prefecture. Exactly 380 encased homesteads developing products of the soil are working in Japan, including some run by gadgets organizations Fujitsu, Toshiba and Panasonic. Be that as it may, what is indoor farming?

Indeed, crops are developed hydroponically (rather than in soil) in a sterile situation with an unequivocally controlled atmosphere. Plants are dribble bolstered supplements and manure through reused water, while sensors can distinguish which supplements are feeling the loss of, this is accuracy cultivating at its generally extraordinary.

Light is given falsely through LED or fluorescent lighting (the previous expending 40% less vitality than the last mentioned), the measure of brightening controlled to augment photosynthesis and breath. In a distribution center in a mechanical park in Indiana, basil, lettuce, kale and chives grow 22 hours every day, consistently every year, lit by a great many blue and red LEDs.

The counterfeit quickening of plant development and growth, accomplished through giving ideal harvest developing conditions, has been believed to build yields by half. At the Mirai lettuce ranch in Japan, lettuces develop twice as quick as those developed outside and are of better quality, containing 8-10 times progressively beta-carotene and 2 fold the amount of nutrient – Vitamin C, Calcium and Magnesium.

Indoor farming likewise offers heaps of different points of interest, liberating makers from concerns, for example, nuisances and maladies, climate and planting times and enabling purchasers to get to new privately developed nourishment throughout the entire year.

They offer shut circle frameworks that procedure plant waste and channel messy water. Some vertical cultivating ventures are utilizing aquaponics whereby squander from cultivated fish is utilized as manure for crops, in this way reusing practically the entirety of the water and diminishing the requirement for manufactured sources of info.

A significantly progressively extreme thought at this point to be completely created is vertical cultivating, basically indoor cultivating in high rises. Such a methodology could spare land enabling previous farmland to be recovered maybe as huge carbon sinks. Obviously this land may not be saved for natural reasons however utilized for different purposes and surrendered farmland may have serious ramifications for farmland biodiversity and country economies.

Changing the Manner in which We Produce Nourishment

As of now it's reasonable there are a few points of interest over present day cultivating. With expanding urbanization (some 70% of the total populace will live in urban areas by 2050), indoor cultivating can help produce nourishment close to where individuals live. It would thus be able to lessen nourishment transportation costs (and related discharges) and conceivably increment urban access to nourishment.

We can create more nourishment in a littler space with less assets, handling area and water asset shortage, environmental change and contamination. One source reports that yields could be multiple times higher than that developed ashore utilizing one tenth of the water. It could likewise empower nations with practically no arable land to develop crops.

In short vertical or indoor homesteads can enable us to:

- Grow nourishment throughout the day, consistently
- Protect crops from capricious and unsafe climate occasions
- Re-use water gathered from the indoor condition
- Eliminate the requirement for pesticides, composts, or herbicides
- Reduce our reliance on petroleum derivatives
- Prevent crop misfortune because of transportation or capacity
- Stop farming overflow

But, there are a few significant disadvantages.

Right off the bat, indoor homesteads for the most part develop leafy foods in spite of the fact that organizations are investigating adjustments to the framework that will enable them to grow a more extensive assortment of harvests.

Rice plants, for instance, are being developed at an indoor paddy field in Tokyo at the Pasona O2. Yet, indoor ranches are probably not going to have the option to develop harvests, for example, potatoes, maize and other subsistence crops. Given that they produce high-esteem crops utilizing refined innovations, to a great extent in created nations, their utilization and incentive in expanding worldwide access to nourishment is dubious.

A few conceivably unsafe theoretical effects could emerge from far reaching reception of indoor cultivating, for example, the translocation of nourishment generation to urban areas causing a downturn in rustic economies, territories where a considerable lot of poor people and hungry live; diminished access to solid nutritious nourishment for provincial networks; and a worsening of the gap between those who are well off and the poor, where innovative headways keep less fortunate nations from joining the indoor cultivating unrest.

When seen as a mechanical answer for the inefficiency and unsustainability of cultivating in the western world, indoor cultivating is hard to condemn. In any case, as the world turns out to be increasingly associated, modern and market improvements in a single nation have significant effects for other people, impacts that we should be substantially more mindful of.

At present creation costs for indoor farming are higher than under customary, tending to utilize greater power. Be that as it may, new advancements are evolving this. Driven lighting has altogether diminished vitality use and has descended generously in cost. Driven lights likewise radiate less warmth, along these lines less cooling is required, lights can be situated nearer to the plants and harvests can be developed all the more thickly.

Another disadvantage to indoor cultivating is that produce will in general be expensive. For instance, the Wall Street Journal found that a head of lettuce from an industrial facility can be multiple times costlier than its open air partner. In the long haul with indoor ranches creating more significant returns in a progressively productive way, economies of scale may serve to decrease costs however for the present indoor cultivating is particularly a rich nation industry.

Indoor farming, regularly alluded to as indoor planting, can be utilized on both little and enormous scales, in home and industrially. Be that as it may, indoor cultivating has a specific fame in huge urban areas where plots of land, in any size, are not promptly accessible for developing and cultivating.

On a huge scale, indoor cultivating is being utilized to help reinforce neighborhood nourishment supplies and give new produce to networks in huge urban communities. A significant number of these ranches are vertical homesteads and can deliver substantially more yields in a little region than can be created in open air, soil-based homesteads. Be that as it may, not every indoor homestead is based on such an enormous scale. Some indoor ranches can be made in a region as little as a cellar and utilized by a solitary nursery worker to give new create to their home.

Most indoor cultivating utilizes a mix of hydroponics and fake lighting to give plants the supplements and light they would possibly get when developed outside. In any case, some indoor cultivating strategies, similar to those executed in nurseries, can utilize a blend of characteristic and fake assets.

When developing inside, numerous indoor ranchers value having more command over nature than they do when they are utilizing conventional cultivating techniques. Light sums, sustenance levels, and dampness levels would all be able to be constrained by the rancher when they are developing harvests exclusively inside.

Albeit developing plants inside can constrain developing choices, cultivators and ranchers have a wide assortment of plants to look over when choosing what to develop inside. The absolute most prevalent plants developed inside are normally crop plants like lettuce, tomatoes, peppers, and herbs.

Indoor farming

CHAPTER 2

Agricultural Conditions Now

Today, agribusiness is at the focal point of huge numbers of our worldwide difficulties. At indoor farms, we started with the basic conviction that innovation is basic to creating both a versatile and supportable answer for those worldwide issues.

The current nourishment production network has a great deal of wasteful aspects. Since we are situated close to the point of utilization, we cut out a great part of the waste and cost in dispersion while conveying a fresher, better item. Simultaneously, the innovation that is utilized in indoor farming enables us to develop in a way that is 100x occasions more beneficial than conventional farming on a similar impression of land, which empowers us to keep the expense of our produce focused with natural items developed in the field.

Indeed, we see indoor farming as one of the answers for issues brought about by developing populaces, environmental change, and progressively restricted assets including nourishment and water supply just as ecological debasement.

For one, there just is not sufficient arable land on the planet to bolster the developing populace utilizing the present traditional techniques, and new product loses 45% of its dietary benefit when delivered. At indoor farming, we tackle for this by re-appropriating already unusable modern space to develop crops indoors, closer to the point of utilization, at a rate that is 100x gainful per square foot of land than that of conventional horticulture.

Product is likewise regularly developed in one focal region, delivered to cold stockpiling, at that point driven by means of long stretch the nation over, and lastly moved by last mile shippers to stores. In the
U.S. alone, nourishment trucking is liable for 12.5% of complete discharges.

By finding near the purpose of utilization, we radically limit the carbon impression of nourishment dissemination. In addition, while the farming business utilizes 70% of the world's freshwater and more than 700 million pounds of pesticides in the U.S. alone, we utilize 95% less water than customary farming and definitely no pesticides.

Can Indoor Farming Solve our Agriculture Problems?

Nourishment is key to our lives – that is guaranteed – yet our association with it is hazardous. Horticulture is one of the main sources of environmental change. With the total populace developing quickly in the following not many decades, the worldwide interest for nourishment is relied upon to increment by 70%.

Nevertheless, the generation of this nourishment is exorbitant: meat and dairy have the most elevated worldwide carbon impression and horticulture utilizes 70% of the world's freshwater, to give some examples hazardous angles. This combined with a more popularity and weight from the impacts of environmental change makes an endless loop. How would we break it?

Indoor farms utilize a hydroponic framework, requiring 95% less water than conventional horticulture to develop produce. Moreover, indoor farming requires less space, implying that it is multiple times more gainful than a customary farm on a similar measure of land. Since the farms are indoors, in firmly controlled conditions, there is additionally no requirement for pesticides.

What Separates Indoor from Conventional Farming?

While conventional farming techniques squander assets and jeopardize our future nourishment supply, indoor farming enables us to develop even more productively and with less assets. Indoor farms utilize zero pesticides, 95% less water, and are 100x occasions progressively profitable on a similar impression of land than conventional horticulture.

We are likewise ready to grow a wide assortment of harvests twice as quick, more yield cycles every year, and more yield per crop cycles than the field, paying little respect to climate or regularity.

Since we are ready to give reliable conditions to crops - numerous which are hard to develop outside, particularly with changing worldwide atmospheres, there are unlimited potential outcomes to what we can develop at indoor farm.

Also, on the grounds that we're near the purpose of utilization and don't need to stress over developing harvests to withstand long travel separations or timeframe of realistic usability, we can develop increasingly tasty, less commodified crops.

Furthermore, on the grounds that we develop in a totally shut condition, we radically limit the danger of defilement from foodborne disease. In contrast to outside farms, which are defenseless against pollution from animal waste, spoiled groundwater or water system run-off, indoor farms produce is developed in a shut circle indoor framework that recycles sifted metropolitan water free of sullying.

Furthermore, in light of the fact that we control the whole procedure from seed to store, greens are not registered through enormous appropriation and satisfaction focuses that regularly lead to extra introduction to contaminants. Innovation and horticulture are not frequently thought of together.

Horticulture and innovation are generally profoundly interwoven. While numerous individuals consider innovation absolutely computerized, agribusiness is really one of the principal significant human mechanical achievements, and is the reason for the formation of towns, urban areas and developments.

Throughout the years, there has been steady advancement in horticulture, and it has bolstered the development of human populaces through today. Therefore, tech and horticulture have consistently had a cozy relationship.

Indoor Farming Advantages

From practical urban development to boosting crop yield with decreased work costs, the benefits of indoor farming are evident.

Solid Harvests with Maximum Crop Yield

Later innovative advances in the horticulture space enable indoor farms to control each part of developing harvests. Factors, for example, light, moistness, and water would all be able to be unequivocally estimated all year.

Since crops are never again dependent on climate examples, temperatures, or light, this implies produce can be dependably grown day in and day out. As nourishment, generation around the globe should increment by 70% by 2050 to sustain the total populace, indoor farming's capacity to expand crop yields will be significant later on.

Decreased Labor Costs

Work has consistently been an agony point in agribusiness - it is one of the most costly parts of farming and the business is right now encountering a work lack. A study found that 56% of farmers were not able contract every one of the representatives they required eventually over the most recent 5 years. Indoor farming can altogether lessen work needs, and in this manner cost, by utilizing robots to deal with reaping, planting, and coordination.

Streamlined Energy Conservation

Indoor farms are worked to streamline vitality protection by fundamentally lessening water and vitality utilization. Studies show that indoor farms utilize around 70% less water than customary farms, which is key in dry season inclined zones.

Indoor farms utilize something like 70% less water than customary farms.

By utilizing cameras and sensors, the information gathered can enable indoor farmers to improve light, temperature, and stickiness levels to locate the ideal equalization essential in delivering nourishment. Specialists in sensor innovation normally change nature inside indoor farms to build profitability and upgrade the nourishment's taste.

Maintainable, Environmentally Friendly Growth

Indoor farms occupy essentially less land room than customary techniques, which makes it engaging in neighborhood urban farming focuses. The structures can be effectively assembled near enormous city populaces, chopping down the measure of time and travel it takes for produce to arrive at the customer.

With a decreased stockpile circulation chain, nourishment gets to the buyer's table quicker and fresher while additionally lessening its carbon impression on the planet.

Putting resources into Indoor Farming

As somebody concentrated on environmental change contributing, it is hard not to observe the size of capital streams into private indoor farming organizations.

There is a ton to like about applying present day mechanical answers for the issue of nourishment creation. The worldwide populace is extending while the earth is warming up.

Progressively essential science should be finished

People have 12,000 years of experience developing nourishment, however just an age or so worth of experience developing yields indoors. We are as yet advancing up the innovation expectation to learn and adapt, to the degree that there is an absence of good information about fundamental inquiries - looking at crop yields for plants developed outside in soil, inside a nursery, and indoors utilizing hydroponics, for example.

In addition, conventional farming strategies depend on conditions that are not appropriate to indoor farming. Outside, nourishment crops are presented to varieties in precipitation, light and wind, and should contend with different plants to rummage for supplements in factor quality soil while presented to the risk of creature or creepy crawly predation.

The way that indoor farming evacuates the vulnerabilities inborn in nature is a positive, yet by taking plants from their regular territories; we are certainly saying that we comprehend everything about what a plant needs to flourish. We do not. Without that understanding, we are left with overproducing crops that are anything but difficult to develop indoors: lettuce, herbs, and verdant greens.

The recently passed different offers help for research and venture into indoor farms and that is a major positive for the business; however regardless we have further to go. Without setting aside some effort to comprehend the science, however, indoor farming is not probably going to have the option to satisfy its elevated inferred guarantees or speculation valuations.

Indoor Farming is not a pure fantasy; however, it is anything but a lay-up either

The expense of driving LED develop lights is probably the

greatest obstacle an indoor farm must defeat for its produce to be focused with products of the soil from a conventional farm.

Vitality costs are high however brings up that that many are trying different things with utilizing less light to develop crops. Logical work has indicated that just about 6% of accessible daylight is utilized in crop photosynthesis, so there might be methods for developing similar plants with less light.

Driven innovation is consistently improving and eventually, governments around the globe will choose to quit externalizing the expense of transmitting ozone depleting substances. Until that time, in any case, enormous scale indoor farm benefit is probably going to stay low.

Indoor farming offers some extraordinary supportability benefits

While vitality costs are not a lay-up, indoor farming creates tremendous efficiencies in different zones. Water utilization might be radically decreased in light of the fact that a similar water can be reused repeatedly through the equivalent hydroponic framework.

Compost use can be incredibly diminished and herbicides and pesticides for weed and irritation control are pointless. These agrarian synthetic substances – which are routinely over-applied, just to run off into waterways and lakes – are likely liable for everything from sea no man's lands to algal blossoms to kick the bucket offs among pollinating creepy crawly.

Considering in the monetary advantages we appreciate because of clean seas and flourishing pollinators, obviously indoor farming offers genuine incentive to society. For whatever length of time that the cost of carbon emanations and ecological contamination is not estimated unequivocally, however, it will be hard for some individuals to precisely see the advantages.

What has to come is most likely cross breed

In certain situations – the Middle East, for example – a transition to indoor farming is an easy decision. An indoor farm in Saudi Arabia, for example, can utilize sun-oriented vitality to control LEDs requiring little to no effort without concealing out other farmland. At present, all vegetables must be brought into the nation, so having privately developed harvests there would be a major success.

In different topographies, however, the cost of building up an office puts a high bar on development and gainfulness that indoor farms experience experienced issues clearing.

Confronting high capital and working costs, question arises assuming enormous, modern indoor farms can productively turn into the essential wellspring of most US customers' leafy foods at any point in the near future.

In any case, littler, take care of indoor farming establishments on by and by, working farms could create countercyclical harvests and supply a neighborhood option in contrast to nourishment that is typically imported.

For example, a farmer in the upper Midwest could work out hydroponics offices in an old horse shelter or an unused plot of land that would be utilized to develop strawberries available to be purchased in Chicago and Minneapolis grocery stores in January. Berries bring a significant expense mid-winter in this piece of the nation, and selling crisp neighborhood produce into this market could include a pleasant, countercyclical pay stream to the farmer.

The Reason Farming is Moving Indoors

Significant Expenses

The most featured indoor farming's possibilities are privately developed, brisk to-showcase, new produce that can be reaped all year, is free of pesticides, and not influenced by unforgiving climate.

Indoor farming can respond to a considerable lot of the inquiries being posed by the present shoppers about the provenance, maintainability and soundness of the nourishment they eat.

In any case, there have additionally been disappointments. Indoor farms are a profoundly escalated capital consumption. Your lighting framework will be one of your most noteworthy capital expenses. In addition, afterward there is ventilation, cooling, water system and gathering. Commit an error and you will have one expensive overhaul not too far off.

Nevertheless, some indoor farms adopt an alternate strategy. They run modern estimated farms. Outside one immense, dim austere distribution center a warmth fog sparkles off the solid. It is a sharp difference to the cold inside where a fragrance of crisp farm produce hits you right away.

Developing nourishment indoors has been around for quite a long time; however, the business got a kick-start from progresses in the presentation of lower cost LED lighting. Join that with mechanical autonomy, advancements and AI, and you have an industry that is both reasonable and versatile.

Indoor farmers converse with an enthusiasm you would expect of business people with tech world foundations. With populace development and environmental change putting pressure on nourishment generation, they figure they may have answers.

Carbon Footprint

It bodes well to develop transient produce in a similar neighborhood as the shopper - stuff that does not travel well. A great deal of produce - tomatoes, strawberries - are developed for movement, not for taste. It does not bode well to indoor farm nourishment with a long timeframe of realistic usability.

Yet, unique produce presents various difficulties. Where plants are concerned, not all light is made equivalent. Fruiting and blooming yields, for example, tomatoes, strawberries and peppers have various needs.

Lights for these sorts of harvests will commonly be progressively costly, require greater power, and produce more warmth, which means extra cooling. Collecting these yields can be a noteworthy operational expense.

That may likewise ease analysis of the business' carbon impression. In the counterfeit light versus daylight banter, the last regularly has the high ground. Be that as it may, at that point, indoor farmers point to the transportation expenses and waste in conventional horticulture.

The carbon impression concerns are substantial, despite the fact that he anticipates that indoor farms should progressively draw on sustainable power source.

In addition, when you see markets situated in extraordinary atmosphere conditions or island countries where they import a greater part of nourishment, indoor farming could be a suitable alternative.

The indoor farming industry is as yet youthful are attempting to work out the correct plans of action and bearing. The business visionaries do not concede to everything, however they surely concur on this: indoor farming can possibly change worldwide nourishment creation, as we probably am aware it.

Indoor Farming: Future of our Reality Farming

With the worldwide populace set to surpass 10 billion individuals by 2050, the test of giving enough nourishment to everybody in an economical, productive and financially perceptive way is rising irrelevance. Shedding the limitations of regular climate designs, beating transportation challenges and essentially upgrading yields, the developing pattern of indoor farming could be the answer for future nourishment creation.

This potential arrangement is truly developing pattern. An idea that sees the rambling harvest farms of old dense into a lot littler manufacturing plant like destinations where conditions can be streamlined and yields fundamentally expanded.

This office utilizes broad indoor racking to enhance space, when contrasted with an ordinary harvest farm empowering it to be situated on a far littler site and a lot more like a set up urban zone such an area decreases the degree of haulage required to move produce to customers, cutting CO_2 discharges.

Topography aside, the making of controlled conditions conveys numerous advantages. Right off the bat, the procedure of harvest generation is protected from regular climate designs that are exceptionally defenseless to interruption because of our evolving atmosphere.

In an indoor farm, lighting, water and temperature would all be able to be upgraded to evacuate climatic dangers and improve generation rates. That is the reason in spite of being another industry, because of new potential outcomes with information examination, yield enhancements are occurring rapidly.

Indoor farms have a huge number of sensors estimating numerous parameters. From, temperature, to supplement levels. The plants are investigated with cameras and sensors, which screen plant wellbeing progressively. Since plant industrial facilities control nature so successfully, it is significantly simpler to effectively run trials and decipher the information.

Expanding yield by the adjusting of factors, for example, CO2 and moistness levels. That as well as due to having significantly more gathers every year, they have much more chances to explore, gather information and learn. This considers a learning rate that is various extents higher than other developing strategies.

Thus, indoor farms are procuring information architects and sensor masters as a critical level of their workforce. Fabricated reasoning as of now assumes a key job in numerous indoor farm activities.

Regardless of this present, it is still at a beginning time. As sensors keep on getting less expensive and progressively proficient, the open doors for indoor farms increments extensively.

Indoor farms additionally upgrade the degree of supplements that yields get, illuminating the test of finding an adequate degree of appropriate farming area in nearness to a significant urban zone. In numerous examples, the dirt is expelled inside and out, and crops are developed on films on layers where they are splashed with supplement rich arrangements.

Indoor farms can likewise expand the yield of some random plant past what is seen in hydroponic nurseries. In addition, it is not a direct result of their extra developing layers. That is because they have an a lot more prominent temperature, climatic and light control than nurseries. This considers prevalent developing conditions and waste end.

Plants just assimilate certain wavelengths of light. Utilizing LED develop lights permits plant processing plants to utilize explicit light plans custom-made to each plant, improving vitality productivity.

While indoor farms, environment, supplement and light control effectively far outperform current developing techniques. There are numerous chances to expand it further. Plant development is mind boggling and influenced by numerous parameters. There is yet a lot of work to be embraced to comprehend the ideal conditions for plants.

Open air plants use changes in daylight to decide when to develop and blossom. Typically, the earth directs this yet LEDs can discharge various plans of light at various development periods of the plant. These light plans can change a considerable lot of their attributes.

They can be utilized together to build the blossoming segment, decrease the root developing stage and even control how the plant tastes. This permits plant industrial facilities to expand the palatable mass rate fundamentally.

Considerably subsequent to thinking about the benefits of Indoor farming, an inquiry emerges, why indoor farming is not utilized all over the place?

The explanation is, indoor farms do have their confinements and pundits have called attention to two primary worries in which the first is the degree of vitality required to keep up such refined situations and second is number of plants which are ineffectively fit to indoor farms because of low consumable mass rate, as being ill-suited to hydroponics, or being a tall yield.

Discussing the main crucial boundary to have the option to develop each harvest type, which is power. Verdant greens do not require a lot of light to develop as they are made of around 95% water and their consumable mass makes up a large portion of the yield.

Contrast that with rice crop, which gives the most calories around the world, providing 19% of worldwide human calories. It is simply 15% water and has a much lower palatable mass rate. Sadly, developing rice utilizing counterfeit lighting would require around multiple times more vitality than cabbage.

Rice developed in an indoor farm utilizing current innovation would deliver incredibly costly rice and have a critical vitality request. Vitality is the significant limitation for plant manufacturing plants and the staggering element that directs what plants can be developed.

While these worries are legitimate, a few indoor farms

are fueled by inexhaustible innovations and reuse a significant number of their assets. The utilization of vitality effective LED lighting lessens control utilization, while the blue and red shades of light are significantly progressively conservative to run.

The productive LED's run colder, in addition to the fact that this saves power it enables them to be put nearer to the plant without gambling heat harm. This permits plant production lines to fit more levels into a fixed structure stature, expanding impression yield.

Closer situating expands light infiltration into the shade enabling plants to be developed nearer together and expanding outright yield. It likewise lessens light drain and builds light ingestion effectiveness, diminishing vitality necessities.

More noteworthy utilization of intelligent cove materials, more profound entering green wavelength light, and mid-level sound lighting can additionally lessen the all-out vitality necessities. The enhanced yield creation process likewise enables indoor farmers to decrease the measure of water utilized, and numerous indoor farms are served by water reaping frameworks.

Some even gather and reuse the water that consolidates inside the controlled condition itself. This shut cycle approach has the additional advantage of keeping supplements and manures from harming land or being washed in waterways and streams.

Over the most recent couple of years, LED lights have improved impressively. Exceptional units are being grown explicitly for indoor developing and their productivity is foreseen to improve by half in the following decade. It is not simply effectiveness however.

LEDs are progressively fit for conveying a more extensive range of light, taking into account more noteworthy control and yields and Reducing the expense of power, which will empower indoor farms to grow a more extensive scope of items.

Considerably after we decrease the expense and increment the productivity of power use, the worry still survives from unsuited plants development, our subsequent concern with respect to indoor farming.

Since current business outside yields, have no compelling reason to consider these parameters they breed plant assortments that flourish outside and are regularly contrary with indoor farms.

Plant Factories have various needs and require distinctive seed types accordingly. There are many midget assortments of existing harvests that could be used. On the off chance that they can coordinate existing yield quality with a seed improved for short tallness, hydroponics and high palatable mass rate, at that point the vitality prerequisite for supplanting existing harvests could recoil essentially.

Moreover, seeds can be reared for quicker collect cycles, not a prerequisite for most current yields. Numerous present harvests penance rearing for top yield in order to breed for fundamental protections. This is not fundamental for indoor farms in view of their fixed conditions. In contrast to nurseries, they do not have to vent and are run like a tidy up room condition.

These yield enhancements alone can altogether lessen the vitality hole for future harvest types, yet it is by all account not the only improvement accessible. This region has an enormous potential for development, particularly for plant industrial facilities that use hereditarily built seeds.

Quality altering systems are getting a lot less expensive and simpler to execute. This has a great deal of potential for both indoor and open air farming later on. Despite the fact that the expense and accessibility of land for indoor farms in urban territories can demonstrate testing, numerous offices are discovering home in re-purposed dispatching holders, previous production lines, and neglected stockrooms.

To be monetarily feasible soon, plants developed in indoor farms in a perfect world need the accompanying attributes: high palatable mass rate, low plant stature, quickly developing cycles, fit to hydroponic developing short timeframe of realistic usability.

In the event that indoor farming can understand the degree of these enhancements, their future vitality request can be significantly lower and will have the option to supply a lot less expensive items than we see today.

Indoor farming

CHAPTER 3

Science of Indoor Farming

Each plant requires similar center fundamentals: light, CO_2, water and supplements. That is the straightforward part.

Be that as it may, these center fundamentals consolidate with a huge number of extra factors depending not just on what crop you are hoping to develop, yet in addition what you need regarding healthy benefit, visual appearance and taste.

When out of equalization, these elements can likewise catastrophically affect the plant, conceivably causing passing at the outrageous or a lower yield in a most ideal situation. Such factors incorporate temperature and moistness, wind stream, length of developing day and then some.

The capacity of cultivators to control pretty much every component of the formula for development implies that we can really guarantee that each plant arrives at its greatest potential. Be that as it may, every component must be deliberately checked so as to streamline its effect on plant morphology.

Would LEDs be able to Replace the Sun?

Light is one of the most pivotal components for plant development. Outside, the daylight traverses an expansive range from UV through to infrared wavelengths. The green wavelengths are reflected and transmitted more firmly by the plant's leaves than the red and blue wavelengths, which are consumed all the more adequately inside leaves for photosynthesis.

The accessible light range and force will be influenced by topography, climate and seasons. Notwithstanding the center capacity of photosynthesis and development, light can likewise go about as a sign to the plant, urging it to create with a particular goal in mind, for example, to advance more noteworthy leaf mass, produce taller stems or empower blossoming.

Notwithstanding, various plants have distinctive light needs, and they react diversely to the light wavelengths utilized, the length of the developing day and the night time frame. Take blooming for instance: you have brief day and difficult day plants, with both requiring diverse photoperiods to incite ideal development.

In the regular world, plants may likewise need to rival their neighbors for light, supplements and water. This vulnerability and mystery can be evacuated through indoor farming.

Understanding the Light Spectrum

As of late, lighting specialists have found how to viably separate and join diverse light wavelengths. By changing the light range "formula", you have far more prominent power over how plants will develop.

The three significant classes of Growth Spectrum resemble this:
- Regenerative:

To advance leaf inclusion and organic product age.
- Adjusted:

To advance in general development execution.
- Vegetative:

To advance plant structure and leaf mass.

Glaring lights were recently utilized for indoor farming, yet progresses in LED innovation, including their handling capacity with regards to light age, light extraction and re-absorbance, have caused LED to develop lights the most effective item accessible available.

Just as having the capacity to run all day, every day, LEDs offer a more noteworthy degree of control as explicit light plans can be structured inside the three primary development range classes to expand the outcomes for singular harvests. LEDs additionally offer an any longer life expectancy than past lighting innovations and can be produced such that makes them simple to spotless and modest to keep up.

Distinctive light plans can likewise be utilized toward the end phase of development to increment anthocyanin combination and pigmentation in produce like red lettuce, where a green plant would be less speaking to the end client.

Nonetheless, light isn't only basic to expanding development, controlling shading and shortening the cycle from planting to collect. Light additionally oversees the circadian rhythms of bugs, bacterial and contagious pathogens, which might be found in developing rooms. Light can subsequently be utilized to configuration traps to restrict the development of stray creepy crawlies or to keep contagious spores from spreading through the yield.

Warmth and Humidity

Temperature and dampness both can possibly quicken development or ruin a yield and are potentially the two most testing components of dealing with your indoor farm.

Temperature significantly affects the speed of development, close by the physiology of plants. The perfect temperature for a plant relies upon various components, and the right harmony between air temperature, relative dampness and light should be accomplished. The development propensity for the plant likewise impacts this procedure.

Also, as you increment temperature inside a characterized range, you get an expansion in gas and water trade between the plant and nature. At the point when the temperature rises, you increment the loss of water, which is the reason you have to stress over the stickiness of nature despite the fact that hotter air can hold more water.

Moistness impacts photosynthesis. This is because of the requirement for water from plants, which is utilized to keep them cool and hold their cell flexibility. The capacity to hold water is resolved, to a limited extent, by the dampness of the air which can build levels of evapotranspiration.

Dampness likewise impacts the capacity of the stomata to attract carbon dioxide and discharge oxygen and water. An excessive amount of dampness can viably prevent the plant from working on a fundamental level. As the racks of lights filling the developing floor are the significant wellspring of warmth in the office, wind current etc. are vital to diminishing instances of tip-consume and shrink.

Plants require a scope of supplements to develop appropriately, however you should tailor your supplement blend explicitly to the harvest, just as your arranged development cycle, root mass and different factors.

The three fundamental kinds of supplements are nitrogen, phosphorous and potassium, yet calcium, sulfur and magnesium are likewise important. An insufficiency in key supplements can bring about everything from death of the tissue and staining to strange growth so it's urgent that you convey the correct supplements at the correct degree of fixation to the roots at the correct snapshot of the development cycle.

With regards to providing plants with supplements, there are a few strategies and substrates that you can utilize. These can be living substrates (soil, peat) or dormant (non-natural). For a long time to come, water system and conveyance of supplements by means of hydroponics is viewed as the most practical and boundless strategy for indoor farming.

The upside of a recycling hydroponic framework is that we can possibly cut the utilization of water by 90% versus customary farming strategies on the off chance that you re-consolidate and re-utilize the mugginess from the developing condition.

This makes indoor farming a perfect choice for districts where water is rare or costly and encourages indoor farms to do their bit for natural maintainability by decreasing misuse of contributions without settling on yield.

Classifications of Indoor Farming Frameworks

Indoor Farming frameworks can be comprehensively partitioned into two classes – those involving numerous degrees of conventional flat developing stages, and those where the yield is developed on a indoor surface. Housetop glasshouses with traditional, single-level creation, while having a place with the class of urban horticulture and having the potential for proficiency improvement through coordination.

Stacked Even Frameworks

This type of Indoor Farming every now and again adjusts existing business ensured cultivation frameworks. Such frameworks contain numerous degrees of conventional level developing stages. Numerous plant crops, for example, verdant vegetables including lettuce and herbs, tomato and pepper are developed in huge scale glass-houses utilizing hydroponic frameworks.

These can incorporate substrate squares shaped of rock-fleece or comparable materials which give a framework to plant roots and are trickle sustained with an absolutely controlled blend of water and supplements. Then again, plants can be developed in pontoons which drift on the outside of beds of supplement arrangement or utilizing a dainty layer of supplement arrangement in the root.

Such frameworks regularly fuse distribution of the supplement answer for keep up ideal supplement arrangement with extra sanitization/sanitation steps to control potential pathogens. Elective methodologies incorporate aeroponics where the root zone is moistened with supplement arrangement, requiring generally low volumes of water, and aquaponics.

These level developing frameworks can possibly be stacked over one another inside taller structures to shape a indoor farm. This can be accomplished either in glasshouses or in self-contained controlled environment (CE) facilities, here and there alluded to as 'Plant Factories'.

Glasshouses have the advantage of having the option to use daylight for plant development with valuable degrees of lighting being required during times of low light, for instance during winter or shady conditions, or for regions of the framework removed from the glasshouse fringe or concealed by more elevated levels of planting.

CE units, be that as it may, being completely encased, require all lighting to be given, consequently expanding the vitality expenses of these frameworks contrasted with glasshouses, despite the fact that the capacity to protect the office as the dividers are not required to transmit light could counterbalance the expense of warming a glasshouse structure.

So as to limit vitality utilization, progressively effective LED enlightenment can be utilized, with the range of light yield custom fitted to the individual needs of specific harvests. Diminished warmth yield from LED lights versus high weight sodium lights ought to enable nearer situating to the harvest, perfect for stacked development levels in indoor farm offices.

The decision of glasshouse or CE will likewise direct the area of the indoor farming framework. Glasshouses should be arranged in areas giving sufficient irradiance. In urban settings, this could involve a detached structure with a glass or polycarbonate shell, developed starting from the earliest stage.

Be that as it may, with the significant expense of land in urban regions, a more practical methodology might be to expand on top or side of existing structures and spot the glasshouse on the top of city structures or on the other hand as a 'green façade'. CE facilities convey no such area confinements and can be put anyplace with satisfactory space.

Various venturesome organizations are utilizing a scope of abnormal urban destinations for nourishment creation utilizing CE frameworks. Moreover, CE frameworks evacuate issues of regularity by keeping up controlled developing conditions all year and can in this manner possibly increment yield by permitting extra gathers of brief period crops during a yearly cycle or by anticipating the impact of occasional change.

Heterogeneity of developing conditions between levels in Stacked Horizontal Conditions Systems is a potential concern. Angles of temperature, light and different components over the distinctive developing levels may bring about undesirable yield inconstancy.

An investigation of a soilless four level strawberry glasshouse framework found huge contrasts in various development parameters between levels, with plants on the top level demonstrating better return and quality than those on lower levels, thought to be because of the more noteworthy accessibility of photo- synthetically dynamic radiation.

In glasshouse-based frameworks, to endeavor to guarantee that each degree of the stacked framework gets an equivalent portion of light, beneficial fake lighting or a pivoting instrument that moves each level thusly to the highest point of the stack can be utilized to diminish concealing of lower levels and keep up homogeneity of developing conditions for each level.

Stacked flat frameworks will in general be utilized in huge scale business undertakings, developing moderately huge volumes of one or a few kinds of yield (for instance, lettuce, spinach and tropical verdant vegetables). Harvest decision in Stacked Horizontal Systems can be directed by the space accessible between each level, with shorter harvests taking into account a higher number of levels thus conceivably more prominent yield per unit stature of the development framework.

Therefore, littler yields, for example, micro-herbs and spinach, which additionally advantage from quick development, thus augmenting turnover and benefit, are regularly supported for their conservative development propensity. Utilization of stacked levels for taller harvests, for example, tomato and pepper may expect changes to development strategies and yield assortments to accomplish significant returns from shorter plants.

Multi-floor Towers

A minor departure from the idea of Stacked Horizontal Systems is that of Multi-Floor Towers. In this situation, as opposed to the numerous degrees of plant development happening in a similar chamber (glasshouse or CE), the various degrees of planting are situated on various floors of a pinnacle structure as are separated from one another.

This enables various conditions to be kept up for each degree of planting which can enable a more extensive scope of yields to be developed by fitting the states of each level to best suit each harvest. By utilizing a physical division between each degree of planting this methodology is generally fit to CE frameworks. Notwithstanding, in spite of various structures, no Multi-Floor Tower frameworks are right now in presence.

Galleries

An option in contrast to indoor development in Multi-Floor Towers is the utilization of galleries for developing product. This methodology is increasingly fit to generation on an individual or network premise as opposed to business endeavors yet may demonstrate valuable for the individual creation of low-volume harvests, for example, herbs.

Indoor Development Surfaces

Green Dividers

Green Walls contain indoor or slanted developing stages sited in areas, for example, the façades of structures. Potential issues with green dividers incorporate the simplicity of gather of plants high over the ground level, introduction to urban contamination in dividers not secured by a defensive surface and upkeep of an equivalent arrangement of water from the through and through of the divider.

Another thought for the area and measurements of green dividers is that of light accessibility. An ongoing report tried to assess the accessibility of building surfaces in an urban domain.

In view of appraisals of plant light necessities determined from leaf physiological attributes of seven verdant vegetables, the investigation found that façade regions presented to coordinate daylight for at least a large portion of the day gave adequate PAR (Photo-synthetically Active Radiation) to plants with high light prerequisites.

The measure of accessible PAR expanded with building tallness but on the other hand was impacted by façade direction and arrangement, with east-west orientated structures viewed as better for consistent development by keeping away from the impacts of north-south wavering of thesun.

The examination additionally featured a danger of inordinate and maybe harmful PAR levels during the center of the day in certain regions. These discoveries demonstrate promising for the development of vegetables in green dividers however should be reassessed to decide developing conditions in calm urban communities and various scopes.

Cylindrical development units

In this sort of framework, plants are grown one over another around the outside of upstanding tube shaped units lodging a supplement supply (soil or hydroponic substrate) and situated inside a glasshouse or CE facility. A correlation between a Cylindrical development unit and a traditional flat developing surface has been made utilizing lettuce.

The two frameworks utilized hydroponic culture and fake lighting. The examination found that albeit Photosynthetic Photon Flux Density (PPFD) and lettuce shoot new weight diminished altogether from the top to the base of the chamber unit, the Cylindrical Development Unit was as yet ready to create more yield per unit floor territory than the level developing surface.

Extra counterfeit lighting could expand crop consistency in such frameworks. Round and hollow Growth Units have been utilized to develop lettuce, strawberry and a scope of herbs.

Contemplations for Indoor Farming

One of the significant issues as of now confronting Indoor Farming is that of a lack of logical investigations of the yield potential, crop quality, vitality productivity and different parameters of VF frameworks all together for their capability to be appropriately surveyed. Be that as it may, here we abridge a portion of the key contemplations for Indoor Farming frameworks and their suggestions on its potential future achievement.

Yield decision

Yield extend in Indoor Farming frameworks is right now restricted, with most makers overwhelmingly supporting serving of mixed greens leaves and other little verdant vegetables. These yield types are appropriate to development in Indoor Farming frameworks for various reasons.

Their little size enables them to be developed in offices, for example, stacked flat frameworks or tube shaped development units where space, especially in the indoor measurement, is at a higher cost than normal. Little plant size likewise permits a higher number of plants, thus possibly expanded salary, per unit zone evenly.

These yields additionally will in general show quick development and a short time span from germination to gather, expanding the quantity of harvests that can be created in a season, further amplifying benefit. A quick turnover of yields additionally permits expanded adaptability in planting system regarding crop decision and enables producers to more readily adapt to issues, for example, crop misfortune because of malady or nuisance harm.

While some little verdant harvests, for example, culinary herbs and plate of mixed greens would be relied upon to encounter sensibly predictable interest quite a long time after year, cultivators of increasingly 'in vogue' vegetables.

For example, smaller scale greens may should be agreeable to quick changes in crop decision if such yields experience a fast decrease sought after, so as to be supplanted by others. Once more, the short generation cycles of such harvests will demonstrate supportive in such manner.

Examination of the reasonableness of indoor farming for the creation of different harvests may extend produce range and salary, with certain cultivators previously utilizing indoor farming for yields, for example, strawberry. New produce crops including verdant vegetables and delicate natural product speak to higher incentive than item crops and can expand salary from a constrained measure of development unit surface.

Different harvests that are much of the time created in secured agriculture frameworks in Northern Europe, for example, tomato and pepper, could in principle be developed in indoor farming frameworks, anyway their enormous plant measure and generally long development cycles make them less suitable up-and-comers. Also, indoor farming frameworks might be utilized for the generation of non-eatable harvests, for example, fancy blooms.

Financial matters

The beginning up expenses of indoor farming frameworks are viewed as a significant requirement, with site determination of high significance. While VF is typically examined in connection to farming in urban territories, and accordingly should take into consideration higher land costs than in country settings, there is no explanation indoor farming frameworks, especially those that adjust traditional business glasshouse agribusiness, can't be utilized in provincial areas.

This can exploit land that is generally unsuited to open air (unprotected) farming and which generally may stay unused for nourishment generation, for example, squander, drained or substantial metal- defiled ground containing poor or unacceptable soil, or ex-mechanical destinations where the ground surface has been supplanted with cement or block.

The decision of country versus urban area is a significant one. For example, it has been assessed that the establishment of a housetop glasshouse requires a base speculation multiple times higher than that for a regular ground-based glasshouse because of the necessary structure adjustment.

Correspondingly, the decision of glasshouse versus CE frameworks will influence prerequisites thus costs for counterfeit lighting and structure development. Utilization of prior structures for CE facilities ought to nonetheless, lessen arrangement costs versus devoted indoor farming structures.

Dissimilar to numerous other nourishment sources, including item crops, the costs for foods grown from the ground have would in general ascent, which could reflect constrained innovative progressions and economy of scale contrasted with different yields.

High leafy foods costs could permit indoor farm plans to recover costs all the more quickly yet additionally, when joined with fire ready for action expenses may chance costs of produce at last being unreasonably high for some shoppers, comparative with other nourishment sources.

Natural impacts

Indoor farming frameworks are often proposed to offer diminished natural effects contrasted with existing inventory chains, for instance by decreasing vehicle prerequisites through finding generation in urban locales.

In any case, it has been determined that of the complete greenhouse gas (GHG) discharge of nourishment frameworks, creation represents 83%, while transport represents 11%. Moreover, as overwhelmingly littler scale makers, indoor farming endeavors may do not have the expanded vehicle vitality productivity gave by bigger scale thus vitality use per transportation unit might be higher.

Conversely, transport separations will be enormously diminished through urban localization and may prompt a net decrease in transport-related vitality prerequisites. Development of indoor farming faculties will likewise create GHGs by means of building development and vitality use.

Investigations of the vitality use, GHG generation, yield and water utilization of indoor farming frameworks are rare. One investigation of the measurement enhancement of a speculative Multi-Floor Tower plan for lettuce creation with counterfeit lighting, water course and sun powered boards on the rooftop and one façade determined that the sun based boards could give adequate vitality to the lighting and water siphoning necessities of the framework.

Be that as it may, the carbon impression of the framework (CO_2/kg lettuce) was multiple times higher than for customary field-developed yields in the late spring and multiple times higher in the winter

when ordinary vitality sources were utilized. Expanded reception of restoration vitality framework may in this manner increment the feasibility and selection of indoor farming frameworks.

While not an indoor farming framework in the most genuine sense, a reenactment based ecological examination work process has likewise been utilized to demonstrate GHG creation in three urban farming situations – a housetop glasshouse, an incompletely encased housetop farm with lookout windows and side windows and a totally encased urban farm with no characteristic light.

The recreation considered countless generation factors including site, crop, activity model, supplemental lighting, warm contemplations, plant development and water use. The outcomes demonstrated that when creating tomatoes, the housetop glasshouse and mostly encased framework could lessen GHG emanations significantly.

Vitality necessities

As indoor farming requires the utilization of a glasshouse or controlled condition office, so vitality use might be relied upon to be higher than for field-developed yields. A model of yield, water and vitality use for lettuce creation in a speculative temperature-controlled hydroponic glasshouse with beneficial lighting and water dissemination has been determined utilizing building conditions dependent on accessible information.

When contrasted with results determined for customary field creation, the hydroponic glasshouse had a 10 times more noteworthy yield and multiple times littler water prerequisite contrasted with traditional generation. Be that as it may, the vitality requests of the hydroponic glasshouse were around multiple times higher.

Boosting effectiveness in indoor farming frameworks, which likewise as often as possible utilize hydroponic culture, will in this way be critical to their prosperity, in spite of the fact that it ought to be noticed that dirt free development can conceivably build yields up to multiple times contrasted with soil-based frameworks.

CE frameworks, with a higher counterfeit lighting prerequisite will probably require considerably further improvement for their utilization to be across the board. The progressing balance between rural land accessibility and vitality use will probably direct the degree of selection of indoor farming later on.

End and suggestions

Indoor Farming is a rising innovation planning to expand crop generation per unit region of land because of elevated weight on rural creation. By using secured agriculture frameworks, for example, glasshouses and controlled condition offices in blend with various degrees of development surface and additionally slanted generation surfaces, indoor farming is an actually requesting and costly way to deal with crop creation.

Indoor farming along these lines requires a consolidated specialized way to deal with factors including lighting, developing framework, crop nourishment, vitality proficiency, development and site choice. While indoor farming has been appeared to have potential for the generation of a wide scope of yields, the specialized and financial streamlining of indoor farming requires further consideration with extra examination into expanding efficiency and decreasing framework costs being required.

Moreover, indoor farming is at present industry-drove, with countless free new businesses. Financing for inquire about with respect to indoor farming at scholastic foundations is constrained. This thwarts streamlining of the proficiency of indoor farming development frameworks and supply chains through an absence of institutionalization of frameworks as each indoor farming undertaking builds up its own methodology.

It likewise implies that a great part of the information accessible for deciding indoor farming achievability, for example, crop yield, is either founded on business promoting material or guess as opposed to logical examination or is inaccessible in the open segment.

This circumstance requires further examination into the feasibility of indoor farming for helpful sizes of nourishment generation. As a division, indoor farming would profit by extra coordinated effort with the scholarly world so as to understand its latent capacity and decide the probability of indoor farming segment development later on as a strong wellspring of nourishment creation.

Grow Lights for Indoor Farming

In its easiest definition, a grow light is a fake wellspring of light, usually an electric light, which is intended to animate the growth of plants by emanating an electromagnetic range ideal for photosynthesis. Such lights are usually utilized in applications where there is an absence of normal light or extra light is required. State for instance, throughout the winter months, grow lights can be utilized to supply extra-long stretches of light for plant growth. It grows vegetables and natural products grow indoors also.

In huge scale indoor farming activities, grow lights can totally supplant direct sunlight. Be that as it may, grow lights don't generally need to emulate sunlight precisely. In numerous applications, they can outflank sunlight.

Kinds of Grow Lights

There are three fundamental kinds of grow lights accessible for indoor urban farming: Fluorescent grow lights, HPS or HID grow lights, and LED grow lights.

- Fluorescent Grow Lights: Fluorescent grow lights are utilized for growing herbs and vegetables indoors. They are two sorts, including fluorescent cylinders and Compact Fluorescent Lights (CFLs). Fluorescent cylinders come in a wide range of forces.

They last more and are more vitality productive than radiant bulbs, the normal bulbs that have been lighting homes for a considerable length of time. Bright light bulbs are thin and can without much of a stretch fit into little spaces. With respect to drawbacks, they require a weight to control current and the cylinders require a stand, as opposed to an ordinary attachment.

Such prerequisites can add to the expense of establishment. Then again, CFLs have gotten increasingly basic in family unit utilization and not simply in indoor urban farming. CFLs utilize just 20 to 30% of the vitality devoured by conventional glowing bulbs and their life expectancy is six to multiple times longer.

They are by a wide margin the least expensive among each of the three significant kinds of grow lights. One remarkable preferred position with CFL bulbs is they don't transmit overabundance heat, enabling ranchers to keep the lights nearer to the plants. This low warmth include makes it very vitality effective too.

• HPS Grow Lights: High-Pressure Sodium (HPS) lights have grown in prominence and are overwhelming fluorescent cylinders and bulbs. These lights are progressively basic among business and experienced indoor growers and the innovation behind them is entrenched, effectively more than 75 years of age.

The issue with HPS is that it creates a lot of warmth. All things considered, you should keep the lights a decent good way from the plants. They require a lot of speculation to set up and keep up. Hence, HPS isn't suggested for little growers.

- LED Grow Lights: While the beginnings of LED innovation previously developed inthe mid-1900s, the red and blue LEDs ideal for indoor farming started being utilized only before the2000s.

LED grow lights are the most vitality productive among each of the three essential sorts of grow lights. These sources can be put more remote from plants while as yet delivering enough light without expending a lot of vitality.

CFLs are practically half less productive than LED grow lights. The warmth generation by LED grow lights is almost zero. Above all, LED performs best to make an ideal indoor condition to make practically any sort of nourishment.

The expense of LED light bulbs is higher than other two sorts, in any case. Also, laborers working in indoor homesteads need to utilize eye assurance as LEDs can be unsafe to human eyes.

Best Fits Based on Farming or Farmer Type

In the event that you are new to indoor farming, CFL is the best fit. It is broadly accessible in numerous wavelengths, and CFL is ideal for use at all phases of plant improvement. Less warmth created by CFLs too is a decent favorable position for little ranchers.

Be that as it may, on the off chance that you need to grow nourishments in huge scale, LEDs can be great long haul speculation as they are the most vitality effective. The utilization of LEDs can decrease vitality use by up to 70%. From numerous points of view, LED grow lights are route superior to daylight for plants.

The Role of LED Grow Lights

The advances in LED innovation have made it conceivable to make the ideal condition to grow vegetables at an enormous scale with shorter growing cycles and more significant returns. Indeed, LED is turning into the true wellspring of lighting to make the most profitable controlled condition for indoor farming. The advances in LED advances have made indoor development of vegetables very vitality proficient.

While most indoor homesteads use LEDs nowadays, many are yet to totally change over to LEDs because of the generally significant expense tag. Be that as it may, the progressively diminishing costs of LEDs should enable those ranchers to change over to LED as it offers a noteworthy vitality cost sparing.

Things Indoor Farmers Must Know About LED Grow Lights

Lighting is the most significant part of making an ideal indoor farming condition. It tends to be a "represent the deciding moment" choice for your indoor ranch. Thus, it's enthusiastically suggested that you invest enough energy arranging and planning the format of your plants and lights. The utilization of CAD (Computer Aided Design) is enthusiastically suggested. The plan ought to be streamlined with the goal that no light will be squandered.

There are exceptional strategies to build the utilization of accessible light in a room. As white surfaces reflect lights, ensure you have the same number of white surfaces around as it is conceivable. Any light- hued surfaces that reflect lights will work a similar way. Also, you can utilize light movers to appropriate the light to a more extensive zone.

At long last, it is critical to stay up to date with the most recent patterns and advancements as they keep on developing in the indoor farming part. Utilize a methodical methodology, while keeping pen to new chances.

CHAPTER 4

Yields Suitable for Indoor Farming

Most business indoor homesteads produce crops inside structures, depending on light-emitting diodes (LEDs) as the sole light source. Despite the fact that there are some indoor ranches inside nurseries, the inconstancy in light power brought about by concealing from harvests and structures above make difficulties to delivering a uniform yield.

There keeps on being expanding enthusiasm for indoor farming, particularly by business visionaries and administrations of nations that depend on the importation of nourishment crops. In any case, in light of the fact that the expenses to construct and work an indoor homestead are high, just particular kinds of yields are possibly beneficial. This article depicts a portion of the yield attributes that loan themselves to indoor generation.

- Short generation cycle: Considering the significant expenses of delivering crops indoors, crops that can be created in weeks — not months — loan themselves to indoor farming. The more it takes to create a yield, the more noteworthy the power cost for lighting and activity of the warming, ventilation and cooling frameworks, just as the more noteworthy fixed costs (lease, hardware deterioration, and so on) that must be distributed to that harvest.

• High harvestable yield: This alludes to the part of the yield that can be reaped and sold. For crops like lettuce, nearly the whole plant can be sold and in this way, has an extremely high harvestable yield. Conversely, for a yield like tomato, one can just sell the organic products. The vitality used to produce and keep up leaves and stems is basically "lost" in light of the fact that there is no market for those parts of the plant.

• Short stature: Plants that have a minimized developing propensity are progressively reasonable for indoor farming in light of the fact that the separation between developing layers can be generally short. Space is utilized less proficiently with taller yields. Except if the separation between the lights and the plants can be balanced (which is regularly not reasonable), all the more lighting limit is expected to arrive at the plants when they are youthful. As plants develop nearer to the light, the light force at the yield overhang increments, yet in addition turns out to be progressively factor.

• All year request: Productivity typically requires nonstop activity and hence, there must be adequate all year showcase interest for the crop(s) developed. Delivering a similar yield all year is a lot simpler horticulturally, and it enables developing frameworks to be designed and advanced explicitly for that harvest. One can envision turning crops regularly, when the market cost for each yield is most noteworthy, however this makes computerization of the developing and collecting forms troublesome, best case scenario.

- Restricted work: Indoor ranchers frequently report that work is probably the biggest expense. In this way, crops can be "planted and developed" with little work loan themselves to indoor farming. Robotization diminishes work inputs, however it typically requires critical in advance expenses to configuration, buy and introduce.

- Transitory: One of the excellences of indoor farming is the capacity to deliver crops near where they are sold, for example, enormous urban communities. The time span of usability as well as nature of transient yields can be expanded when the period among reap and arriving at the market is short. A short collect to showcase time can likewise lessen shrinkage contrasted and crops shipped long separations.

- High worth: Due to the more prominent expenses of delivering crops indoors, they have to direction a generally significant expense. We can create any nourishment crop indoors, however is the value acquired adequately high to be productive?

- Worth included: It is conceivable to create a more excellent yield indoors contrasted with customary or nursery farming. What's more, crops developed indoors are regularly more solid and uniform than other generation strategies. Extra worth included properties that are conceivable incorporate increasingly nutritious; "better" surface, enhance, and additionally shading; and a more drawn out time span of usability.

Plants that are Perfect for Indoor Farming

Indoor farming is an awesome method to benefit as much as possible from restricted open air space. You can without much of a stretch change a little terrace or overhang into a flourishing foods grown from the ground fix. Past their space-sparing ability, there are extra focal points to indoor nurseries; plants will get a lot more prominent presentation to sun and oxygen and be shielded from many nursery bugs, similar to slugs.

Tomatoes are a most loved among planters of pretty much every stripe. Simple to develop, they do well in a wide scope of plant strength zones. Preparing your tomato vines to grow up an emotionally supportive network of stakes, trellises, or pens limits the nursery space you need, while simultaneously it shields your plants against soil-borne malady.

Peas, both the commonplace and snow peas, appreciate cool temperatures (70 degrees Fahrenheit probably). They needn't bother with a lot of water or compost, yet ought to be furnished with a trellis or posts for climbing.

Cucumbers, zucchini and summer squash are perfect for an indoor nursery on the grounds that these three individuals from the cucurbit family all yield produce which is moderately lightweight and can be upheld by a trellis. An intriguing incidental advantage is that indoor farming this kind of harvest will in general outcome in straighter veggies.

Melons and winter squash species which produce natural product weighing as much as 3 pounds are extraordinary in indoor nurseries. They'll require a solid trellis – planting beside a steel fence is perfect. As it ages, bolster the natural product with a stretchy texture sling (formed from a disposed of T-shirt or pantyhose).

Kiwis are another vine which will change up your indoor nursery. Trellising gives kiwi plants access to the full sun they ache for. Frequently thought of as a tropical natural product, kiwis are really equipped for flourishing.

Hops are a kind of vine which is regularly utilized as an enhancing planting. Be that as it may, the hop organic product is prized as a seasoning operator for brew, while the delicate youthful shoots are filled in as a vegetable in European cooking. Quickly developing hops can arrive at a great 25 feet in tallness and require a durable emotionally supportive network, for example, wooden shafts.

Passion fruit is a tart natural product which, contingent upon the assortment, prefers the warm climate of Zones 6 to 10. Prune the plant all the time to support organic product improvement and watch that it doesn't assume control over your nursery. Regardless of whether enthusiasm natural product is unreasonably astringent for you to eat as seems to be, it's awesome softly improved and made into a straightforward sorbet – have a go at blending in with strawberry or peach for an alternate flavor profile.

Green beans, as pole beans, are easy to become indoor in a little space and have a more drawn out collect season than the bramble assortment, offering you a consistent stockpile of beans for a while. As the name recommends, they climb well on posts. Affix with hemp twine, which can be treated the soil together with your bean vines toward the finish of the developing season.

Corn, okra, Brussels sprouts, and sunflowers are perfect possibility for indoor farming. They normally become indoor and needn't bother with any help. Truth be told, these tall plants would themselves be able to fill in as an emotionally supportive network for lightweight vines.

Greens like **lettuce, kale, and basil** likewise have a spot in your indoor nursery. Verdant herbs and serving of mixed greens lean toward at any rate halfway shade, so you can fold them under enormous sun-adoring plants. Or on the other hand develop them in an obscure corner utilizing indoor grower made from beds, stacked or hanging pots, retires, or garden pockets.

Indoor Farming Systems

These progressive indoor farming frameworks can before long supplant the conventional horticulture systems.

Many have thought about for a considerable length of time whether indoor farming is actually the response to the lack of nourishment on the planet. Anyway weird the idea of indoor farming may appear to numerous new businesses, it is a brilliant strategy to deliver nourishment in situations where arable land is inaccessible or uncommon and no more.

These techniques are particularly convenient for testing situations, for example, deserts, mountainside towns, and urban communities where numerous assorted sorts of vegetables and organic products are developed utilizing exactness horticulture strategies and high rise like structures.

Indoor farming is a progressive and more manageable technique for horticulture than its partner as it brings down the necessity of water to up to 70% and furthermore spares significant space and soil. This development in the field of agribusiness with maintainability as its adage is making an ever increasing number of heads turn today with its eco-accommodating strategies and making the probability of farming genuine in troublesome environs.

Hydroponics

Hydroponics is a transcendent arrangement of developing that is utilized in indoor farming, and it is gradually yet consistently, picking up significance. It includes around the development of plants in arrangements of supplements that are basically free of soil.

In this indoor farming advancement, the underlying foundations of the plants are submerged in an answer of supplements. This is regularly circled and observed so as to guarantee that there is the upkeep of the right compound structure in the supplement arrangement.

Hydroponics is a subset of hydroculture, the technique for developing plants without soil, utilizing mineral supplement arrangements in a water dissolvable. Earthly plants might be developed with just their foundations presented to the mineral arrangement, or the roots might be bolstered by an

idle medium, for example, perlite or rock. The supplements in hydroponics can be from fish squander, duck fertilizer, or ordinary supplements.

Hydroculture is the developing of plants in a soilless medium, or an oceanic based condition.

Hydroponics is the study of developing plants without soil- - in spite of the fact that the plants could conceivably be suspended in a strong medium, for example, rock, or extended mud balls.

Soil holds minerals and supplements, which "feed" vegetation, as we as a whole know. Plant roots can't assimilate earth, be that as it may; when water goes through soil, it breaks down and gathers a portion of the supplement particles implanted. This "nourishment" arrangement is absorbable as a fluid.

As should be obvious, the dirt itself isn't a necessary piece of a plant's nourishing cycle - it is essentially a stabilizer for the roots, and an advantageous channel. Plants inhale air, much the same as people. Younger students are shown a straightforward exercise: plants take in carbon dioxide, and discharge oxygen.

The whole plant - not simply verdant material- - adds to this procedure. If not appropriately kept up, soil can hold an excess of dampness, adequately choking or suffocating a plant's root framework. On the other hand, if the dirt doesn't contain enough dampness, the plant will be not able retain the supplements it needs to endure.

The underlying foundations of a hydroponic plant have consistent access to both air and water, and it very well may be a lot simpler to keep up that equalization since the roots are commonly unmistakable.

The normal plant needs at any rate five things to endure. Air, water, supplements, minerals, and light. Inasmuch as you can give these things in bounty, your plants should remain sound.

Developing your very own nourishment can be a compensating experience. On the off chance that your hydroponic framework is indoors, you can develop nourishment during the off-season as well. You'll likewise get a good deal on without pesticide produce and realizing your nourishment wasn't dispatched from a third-world ranch that might be supporting terrible strategic policies, similar to cultivate specialist misuse

Despite the fact that a bit much for the endurance of a plant, substrate can bolster a plant physically and hold it upstanding, either by verifying the root framework, or by exceeding the plant itself.

There are numerous sorts of substrates monetarily accessible. Check your nearby nursery or home improvement shop.

On the other hand, there are bounty to be discovered outside, particularly close to waterways. Indeed, even basic stone can adjust the PH of your framework. While checking your PH balance, make certain to check it after it has flowed through your substrate.

In the dampness rich conditions hydroponics regularly give, substrate can be commonly ordered into the accompanying classes: sandy, granular, and pebbled.

Sandy situations comprise of particles between .06 (fine) and 2mm (coarse) in width. Indeed, even coarse sand holds a lot of water (with the exception of in contrast with soil), and isn't commonly viewed as suitable for use in a hydroponic framework. In the event that you utilize a siphon, for instance, the little molecule size may prompt stop up.

In any case, it is modest and promptly accessible, and, when wet, is sufficiently substantial to give a sensible grapple to plant roots. There is some absorbable supplement in sand. Commonly, the supplements inactive in sand culture shift generally on the substrate's shading and cause. Most sand contains a huge amount of shell parts, and in this manner has a high calcium content.

Dark sand as a rule has a high magnetite content starting from volcanic stone, known for its fruitfulness. Orange or yellow sand may be a pointer of a high iron substance. White sand will in general be extremely high in silica, which helps manufacture solid cell dividers in plant life.

Granular particles run somewhere in the range of 2 and 4mm. This may comprise of rock, or plant mulch. Stone rock makes an overwhelming, non-biodegradable stay for plant roots, and is energetically suggested for use in hydroponic frameworks. Stone rock contains next to no dormant plant sustenance, much the same as sand. There are a few evaluations of rock promptly accessible to browse.

Spring rock and Pea Gravel comprise of round, sparkling stones. The smooth state of these stones takes into consideration incredible air circulation and root development, in spite of the fact that the seepage might be over the top. Squashed stone is regularly made by smashing enormous lumps of limestone or dolomite into little pieces.

Squashed stone has more keen edges than spring rock, and will in general interlock better. This more tightly weave makes for higher water maintenance, in spite of the fact that limestone will in general gauge less. Limestone is a solid soluble base. Check your PH, and parity likewise.

Stone-based substrate is profoundly re-useable. It is impressively less chaotic than sand to bubble for cleansing. In the event that weight isn't a worry (i.e.: the plants you develop are not expected to arrive at extensive statures) you should think about utilizing a plant mulch, for example, peat mulch, cedar shavings, or coir (coconut peat).

Mulches hold a high amount of water, yet in addition inhale well indeed. Mind you, they are likewise profoundly degradable, which can prompt obstructed siphons, and wood shavings frequently contain sweet-smelling oils which can repress plant development. Shape and green growth development represents a higher hazard when mulches are included, yet present one extensive bit of leeway over rough substrate: they can be treated the soil and supplanted with new material.

It shouldn't be put away. I wouldn't recommend re-utilizing them, in any case. This is particularly advantageous on the off chance that you utilize hydroponic frameworks solely to begin seeds, or develop during the off-season.

Pebbled substrate quantifies somewhere in the range of 4 and 64mm. Stone rocks have the essential attributes of brook rock. They are normally smooth, frequently glossy, and the holes between the stones make for low water maintenance and high air circulation. The shinier the stone, the more terrible the water maintenance will be.

A matte or blemished surface shows a permeable stone, which will remain damper, longer, while as yet giving incredible air circulation. Stones - particularly the permeable assortment - can detonate when warmed for sanitization.

You should heat up your substrate between utilizations to disinfect it. Microorganisms love warm, wet conditions and will likely flourish in a hydroponic framework. Green growth cherishes wet and warm frameworks, as well, and it can look unattractive.

On the off chance that you care about appearances, heating up your substrate between utilizations will debilitate blooming, however on the off chance that you utilize dim (reused from past use) water you'll be taking on a losing conflict.

Lettuce enhances the water with nutrients and minerals required for development and wellbeing of the plants, alongside controlled for ideal outcomes, for example, temperature, light, dampness, and so forth. This system requires severe wellbeing methods and sanitation.

Maintaining a strategic distance from the misuse of water through reuse, disposing of the utilization of herbicides and fungicides and significantly decreases the utilization of pesticides. At the point when every one of these conditions are joined, the lettuces are increasingly delicate, less sinewy than ordinary farming techniques.

V love cultivates that can supply lettuce with its underlying foundations unblemished. Conveying crisp lettuce with roots still connected gives dampness and supplements a chance to keep on providing sustenance. Developed in a nursery utilizing no pesticides or herbicides, heavenly!

Aquaponics

An Aquaponics System is a lot of like the Hydroponics System however is just better. It expects to consolidate the fish and plants in a similar biological system. In this framework, fish develop in indoor lakes and produce a supplement rich waste that further goes about as a nourishment hotspot for the plants developed in indoor ranches.

The plants, doing their part, cleanse and channel the wastewater that gets reused legitimately to the fish lakes. Aquaponics is certainly utilized at a littler scale than most indoor farming developments.

In any case, it is as yet utilized by numerous business indoor ranches that desire to create only a couple of quickly developing harvests as opposed to including the part of aquaponics. Subsequently, the creation and financial aspects issues are rearranged and it additionally boosts proficiency.

All things considered, this shut cycle framework may turn out to be increasingly famous with the prevalence of new institutionalized aquaponics frameworks.

Aquaponics alludes to any framework that consolidates traditional aquaculture (raising oceanic creatures, for example, snails, fish, crawfish or prawns in tanks) with hydroponics (developing plants in water) in an advantageous situation. In ordinary aquaculture, discharges from the creatures being brought can gather up in the water, expanding harmfulness.

In an aquaponics framework, water from an aquaculture framework is sustained to a hydroponic framework where the results are separated by Nitrifying microscopic organisms at first into nitrites and hence into nitrates, which are used by the plants as supplements, and the water is then recycled back to the aquaculture framework.

Eatable Seaweed are green growth that can be eaten and utilized in the planning of nourishment. They regularly contain high measures of fiber and are a finished protein. They may have a place with one of a few gatherings of multicellular green growth: the red green growth, green growth, and darker green growth.

Carrageenan are a group of straight sulphated polysaccharides that are separated from red eatable ocean growth. They are generally utilized in the nourishment business, for their gelling, thickening, and balancing out properties. Their fundamental application is in dairy and meat items, because of their solid authoritative to nourishment proteins. There are three principle assortments of carrageenan, which contrast in their level of sulphation. Kappa-carrageenan has one sulfate bunch for each disaccharide, Iota-carrageenan has two, and Lambda-carrageenan has three.

Wetland reclamation is basic for improving biological

system administrations, yet numerous oceanic plant nurseries don't have offices like those ordinarily utilized for enormous scale plant generation. This investigation endeavors to figure out what techniques would adequately profit the enormous scale generation of amphibian plants as a potential asset of reinforcing the improvement of the biological systems.

Aquaculture

Aquaculture is the farming of fish, scavengers, mollusks, sea-going plants, green growth, and other sea-going life forms. Aquaculture includes developing freshwater and saltwater populaces under controlled conditions, and can be appeared differently in relation to business angling, which is the collecting of wild fish. Mariculture alludes to aquaculture rehearsed in marine situations and in submerged natural surroundings.

Algaculture is the farming of types of Algae, which is a casual term for an enormous, assorted gathering of photosynthetic living beings which are not really firmly related, and is in this manner polyphyletic. Included living beings go from unicellular genera, for example, Chlorella and the diatoms, to multicellular structures, for example, the monster kelp, an enormous darker alga which may grow up to 50 m long.

Most are oceanic and autotrophic and need a significant number of the particular cell and tissue types, for example, stomata, xylem, and phloem, which are found in land plants. The biggest and most complex marine green growth is called ocean growth, while the most mind boggling freshwater structures are the Charophyta, a division of green growth which incorporates, for instance, Spirogyra and the stonewort.

Microalgae

Microalgae is the base of the nourishment web and give vitality to all the trophic levels about it. Microalgae biomass is regularly estimated with chlorophyll a fixations and can give a valuable record of potential creation. The standing supply of microphytes is firmly identified with that of its predators.

Without brushing pressures, the standing load of microphytes drastically diminishes.

Microphyte, which are Microscopic Algae, commonly found in freshwater and marine frameworks living in both the water section and dregs. They are unicellular species which exist exclusively, or in chains or gatherings. Contingent upon the species, their sizes can go from a couple of micrometers (μm) to two or three many micrometers.

In contrast to higher plants, microalgae don't have roots, stems, or leaves. They are uncommonly adjusted to a situation commanded by gooey powers. Microalgae, fit for performing photosynthesis, are significant for life on earth; they produce roughly 50% of the climatic oxygen and use at the same time the ozone harming substance carbon dioxide to develop photo autotrophically.

Ocean Lettuce a gathering of palatable green growth that is broadly appropriated along the shorelines of the world's seas. The sort species inside the family Ulva will be Ulva lactuca. Lactuca being Latin for "lettuce". The family additionally incorporates the species recently arranged under the sort Enteromorpha, the previous individuals from which are known under the basic name green nori.

Nori is the Japanese name for eatable kelp types of the red green growth family Pyropia, including P. yezoensis and P. tenera.

Small Scale Greens

Small scale Greens is a minor vegetable green that is utilized both as a visual and flavor segment or fixing principally in fancy eateries. High end food culinary specialists use microgreens to upgrade the magnificence, taste and freshness of their dishes with their sensitive surfaces and particular flavors.

Littler than "child greens," and collected later than "grows," microgreens can give an assortment of leaf flavors, for example, sweet and zesty. They are likewise known for their different hues and surfaces.

Among upscale markets, they are currently viewed as a forte classification of greens that are useful for embellishing servings of mixed greens, soups, plates, and sandwiches.

Consumable youthful greens and grains are delivered from different sorts of vegetables, herbs or different plants. They extend in size from 1" to 3" including the stem and leaves. A microgreen has a solitary focal stem which has been cut simply over the dirt line during gathering.

It has completely created cotyledon leaves and for the most part has one sets of extremely little, halfway grew genuine leaves. The normal yield time for most microgreens is 10–14 days from seeding to collect.

The Amount to Grow

Growing is the act of developing seeds to be eaten crude or cooked. Sprouts can be developed at home or created modernly. They are an unmistakable element of the crude nourishment diet and basic in Eastern Asian cooking. Growing, such as cooking, decreases hostile to wholesome mixes in crude vegetables.

Crude lentils for instance contain lectins, antinutrional

proteins which can be diminished by growing or cooking. Growing is additionally applied on an enormous scale to grain as a piece of the malting procedure. A drawback to devouring crude sprouts is that the way toward developing seeds can likewise be helpful for destructive bacterial development.

Germination

Shoot comprise of stems including their limbs, the leaves and horizontal buds, blossoming stems and bloom buds. The new development from seed germination that becomes upward is where leaves will create. In the spring, enduring plant shoots are the new development that develops starting from the earliest stage herbaceous plants or the new stem or blossom development that develops on woody plants.

In ordinary discourse, shoots are frequently synonymous with stems. Stems, which are a vital part of shoots, give a hub to buds, organic products, and leaves. Youthful shoots are regularly eaten by creatures in light of the fact that the filaments in the new development have not yet finished auxiliary cell divider advancement, making the youthful shoots gentler and simpler to bite and process.

As shoots develop and age, the cells create auxiliary cell dividers that have a hard and extreme structure. A few plants (for example bracken) produce poisons that make their shoots unpalatable or less satisfactory.

Conclusion

Indoor farming could help increment nourishment creation and extend agrarian tasks as the total populace is anticipated to surpass 9 billion by 2050. What's more, by that equivalent year, two out of each three individuals are required to live in urban territories.

Delivering new greens and vegetables near these developing urban populaces could help satisfy developing worldwide nourishment needs in an ecologically mindful and supportable manner by decreasing dissemination chains to offer lower emanations, giving higher-supplement produce, and radically lessening water use and overflow.

Quickly developing conurbations specifically can profit: transportation costs are constrained in light of the fact that vertical homesteads are frequently situated in urban communities, near the purchaser. Because of the low sending costs it likewise has potential for disconnected areas like remote islands, while the controlled developing condition makes it promising for territories with extraordinary atmospheres, for example, deserts.

Be that as it may, indoor farming frameworks are probably not going to get aggressive inside the following not many years for the enormous scale generation of agriculture crops in nations like the Netherlands. That is for the most part since (potential) urban ranchers face a moderately high introductory speculation and soak power bills.

Truth be told, indoor cultivated vegetables (mostly verdant greens) cost about twice as a lot to develop as a similar harvest delivered in a nursery.

Over every one of the contentions, indoor farming has become undeniably increasingly famous lately, as innovation has gotten significantly progressively exact, permitting a lot of greens and crisp produce to be created in urban situations with both insignificant space and far littler measures of water than on a conventional ranch.

Indoor farming

books recommended to young entrepreneurs that I liked

- *Frank Dalton: **The force of anger**: turn your anger into self-motivation and positive energy*
- *Frank Dalton: **Hello, Talent! We can finally meet!**: Everyone has a talent, even if he doesn't know It*
- *Frank Dalton: **From introversion to leadership**: a guide for defeating the limits of introversion and shyness, and becoming a great leader*
- *Frank Norving: **You are your business**: How to be a great businessman starting from zero*
- *Frank Norving: **Be a business general**: The secrets of teamwork in business, and why you should lead your business from the front*
- *Demetra Harlington: **Meditation to develop Talent**: Unlock your talent with Meditation*
- *Demetra Harlington: **Meditation for a Leader**: Meditation to Increase Happiness. Finding Mindfulness at Work. How to Live Stress-Free and in the Moment*
- *Manuel Honner: **Your best skill: being creative**: How to recognize and show up creativity, the best skill you don't know to have*

www.ingramcontent.com/pod-product-compliance
Lightning Source LLC
Chambersburg PA
CBHW050554160726
48003CB00002B/888